A Brief History of Trees

By Lawrence Illsley

Lawrence Illsley is an award-winning poet originally from Cornwall. His first collection Astra and Sebastian (Proverse 2011) was shortlisted for the Proverse Prize. Find him on instagram @abriefhistoryoftrees or on twitter @Lawrence_poet

First Published in 2020
By Live Canon Poetry Ltd
www.livecanon.co.uk

© Lawrence Illsley 2020

978-1-909703-96-4

Contents

Acknowledgements:

I would like to thank: my sister Rachael for her encouragement and insight and, who with Dan and Titus, shared it all with me. Hannah Copley, Toby Litt and Julia Bell for their early support and insightful editing. My Birkbeck workshop group, Katie, Laurane, Miki, Kayleigh, Alex, Tabitha, Goran, Aine and Jane for discussion and friendship. My friends Ben, Shane, Tom, Ollie and Sam for their kind words, help and hospitality. Martin Stansbury for his vision. And finally, Helen Eastman, Glyn Maxwell and all at Live Canon for giving this poem life.

For mum, and Caroline, who helped me through it.

... You said you'd like to come back as a tree,
but never said which you would like to be...

1. A mother beech, Tregeseal

That August we sat in chairs, not moving.
      Both of us absorbed. Reading old fiction
            or watching television. The hovel
                 you called it. But it was home. More than room

enough. Sometimes I wrote and foliage
      would appear in my mind. Every scene
            seemed to require a green backdrop of trees.
                 Although the wildwood of another age

has long been stripped - for ships' masts, or lathes
      for plaster; for Bronze Age fires to cast swords;
            fences to restrain pigs and sheep; wide boards
                 and planks for walls and drawers; swathe

            after swathe cut, planed and sawed - lone trees still
      survive, gracing the landscape. To describe
            our windswept world requires knowledge. How I'd
                 not got sufficient vocabulary

at past thirty-five to identify
      more than a handful of trees, a small copse,
            bothered me. Whilst waiting in hospital
                 for the nurse to do your endoscopy,

I didn't idly skim magazines from
      last year, or leaflets on Stannah stairlifts.
            I read books on trees - mapping out visits
                 to local woodlands, clifftops and valleys.

I had a hunch that something serious was happening.
      You wouldn't eat. Yet, I wasn't prepared
            for those days to be our last together.
                 It was so lucky how everything

worked out. That I took a break to write
in the country. See the Cornish summer:
Trewellard, Porthcurno, Cot, Porthgwarra,
and you for the first time in years.

To spite me, there was fog. Thick pea-soupers
immersed the village in grey miasmic
drifts. Walkers, tourists and the fantastic
views covered by water. You were used to

this. But I found it oppressive. Almost
depressing. The clouds malign. A challenge
to survive. We lit fires. Red and orange
flames consumed coal in your black grate. The ghosts

of carboniferous ferns and horsetail,
one hundred foot tall, that died in stagnant
swamps, three hundred million years extant.
Crushed in that time to coal. Our woodland will

never become coal. It lacks the carbon
rich humus. The soil is too poor. Humans
are the difference. Centuries of cutting
and burning down trees has changed the system.

The sea had disappeared from your windows.
On sunny days, the white-maned Atlantic
rode unbroken to the skyline. Granite
cliffs genuflecting bent to the ocean.

So I walked - wrapped in old waterproofs
and inappropriate shoes - down wet tracks,
past the pay-and-display car park and plaques
describing ruined mines, to smell the salt,

and see the waves from the cliffs at Levant.
        The mist was down. Damping all sound.
                Near to the edge, I came out of the clouds,
                        and a quicksilver sea stretched, infinite

and glassy, three hundred feet below me.
        A molten glass lake on an alien
                planet. The clouds above, a grey, gauze screen.
                        Water above water. Hung. Suspended.

On the prow of the headland I noticed
        a wave carved tunnel I had never seen
                before. Then I saw a shaft in the scree
                        on a ledge below. I couldn't resist

and scrambled down. A metal spherical
        grate, some twenty feet in diameter,
                capped the black depths of a granite chasm.
                        The sea far beneath. Thrashing and brutal.

Clawing at the rocks. I took a deep breath
        and walked out upon the grate to see if
                I'd die. A local boy lost in the mist.
                        In ten steps. Feet ringing on the metal

                rungs. The drop sucking at my shoes. I was
        done. Safe on the other side. Breathing hard
but alive. On another walk, by the
                river in Tregeseal valley, it all

got too much for me and I had to phone
        Rachael to tell her that I was worried
                you weren't eating. That I'd postpone my master's
                        and stay in Trewellard till it'd blown

over. That the novel wasn't moving
        forwards. She calmed me down. We decided

I was panicking. A typical side
        effect of staying at yours for too long.

The road was grey-green. Running
    through a tunnel of sycamore. The light
        dim. A crepuscular valley. Shelter
           from the incessant mizzle seeping

that day from the monochrome emulsion
    of the cloud-smeared sky. Broadleaved trees, other
        than sycamore, are rare there. They cower
           in the narrow valleys. Or the odd lone

tree will grow up from a hedgerow. Branches
    raked across the sky by the wind. Further
        along the valley - by the waterworks
           and the old wooden bridge we played on as

youngsters - I found a solitary beech
    on the riverbank. Its oval leaves, like
        those children draw in school, identified
it immediately. Closer. I reached

out a hand and touched it. Beech do better
    in woods surrounded by their kin. Not stood
        all alone. But this one had taken root
           despite the isolation. A clutter

of hairy cupules - last season's flowers
    grown woody after pollination - lay
        like a thick rug over its feet. Humans
           once foraged this nutritious mast. Wedded

to the weather and fearful of frost, beech
    were chased south by glaciation in the
        Pleistocene. They waited in Italy
           near the Mediterranean beaches

for the ice to retreat. Not to be rushed,
        a sedate breeze blew their seeds north across
                the chaste Alps, over damp Doggerland,
                        arriving in England in six thousand

BC. Just before the glacial melt
        water flooded the channel creating
                an island. An island full of trees. Lime,
                        oak and elm had already formed vast woods.

Hazel underbrush covered the ground. Beech
        shoots popped up and waited. A beech is used
                to waiting. Born into shade in beech woods
they wait for light. In stealth they grow. Reaching

        slowly for the sky. Two hundred years as
                a sapling perhaps, until an old tree
                        falls leaving a gap in the canopy.
                                Slowly they conquered Kent and the south-east

and now they rule England. Queen Beech. Nature's
        cathedrals. Cloaked in green. Togetherness and
                connection seem important to beech trees.
                        Their supple branches graft to a neighbour's,

forming a chorus line on the hedgerow.
        Whilst underground, their network gets complex.
                A forest talking in slow electric
                        pulses. Root to root. Sharing nutrients

through a wood-wide-web of mycelium
        strands. Mycorrhiza fungus down in the
                rhizosphere connects kin so that mother
                        beech can feed their progeny. Helping them

to grow strong in the dark. In Old English,
the beech was called bōc, which became the word
book, just as leaves became pages.
Nothing on the endoscopy.

Yet, still you complained of feeling queasy.
So, we went up to Sainsbury's to buy
Complan and a kettle. Yours had broken.
Back at the house I tried to get you to talk.

But in vain. Silence had been your
companion for too long. Instead I sang
songs on my Spanish guitar that wouldn't
stay long in tune. You smiled and asked for more.

Your doctor was baffled. She booked a scan
in Penzance. As we waited, we chatted
about me graduating from my degree and
whether I should head back to London to
continue my studies.

Go, you said. *I'm fine. Soon
I'll be better. But I can't come to Brighton
for your graduation ceremony.*

I don't feel like travelling. So sorry.

2. A Cornish elm, Brighton

Brighton was sun-kissed. I rolled my shirt sleeves
        up and the ice cream flowed. The brash seafront
                sparkled. I queued for my robes. We ate lunch
                        on the beach as a pearlescent blue sea

lapped on ochre pebbles. Rachael came down
        from Bristol with Titus. We hung out. Laughed
                over beers. Took albums of photographs
                        of us all playing and me in my gown.

We WhatsApped them all straight over to you,
        and waited patiently for your reply.
                Later that afternoon, my cloaked body
                        sweating in the packed auditorium,

I clapped the other graduates until
        my hands smarted. Then I walked on the stage.
                Shook hands with the Dean. Gave the room a wave,
                        and thought how I had finally fulfilled

your expectations, only fifteen years
        later than planned. I'd always imagined
                you'd be there. Cheering in the crowd.
We fled to Worthing - bits of Mr. Potato

        Head all over the back seat of the car -
                and checked into our Travelodge hotel.
                        I went to Rachael's room and watched the swell
                            through the window. I felt avuncular

as Titus played hide and seek. When you phoned,
        I dropped the curtain. Sat. And we chatted.
                Rachael filmed Titus. You cried. The lattice
                        of the lace curtain blurred the tide-washed stones

of the beach. You rarely cried. Though drinking
    hock made you maudlin. You told me how kind
        the neighbours were. You never wanted to
            be old. You'd nursed too many people through

the leprous drag that precedes modern death.

Including dad, your man. Who didn't go
    quickly or gently into that good night.
        But expired all the same. Were you frightened
            that day? Did you know? I promised to phone

you from London later on in the week.
    We ate some dinner at Pizza Express
        and went to bed early. But I couldn't rest.
            The ocean was too close. Beckoning me.

I grabbed a can of beer from my bag and
    walked onto the beach. The water was black.
        Bituminous and thick. Barely a kink
            in it. Strange invisible ink. The land

unstained by each soft wave's tentative lap.
    I stripped off. It was dark. The beach empty.
        The water rose past my thighs. My belly
contracted as the cold first bit. Then wrapped

        me. I dove into the shadows, swimming
            until warm, then lay, floating on my back,
        looking at the starlight pricking the dark
foliage of the night's domed crown. My skin

dissolved. I felt part of the watery
    planet I walk on each day. Lightning flashed
        near the bowed horizon. The skeletal
            frame of a tree, unleaved, hung in the sky.

Luminescent in the electrified

air. A summer storm flayed the vast, saline
plain, but I watched on, unharmed.
The next day, the Brighton
to London train was delayed

so I walked up to Preston Park to find
a Cornish Elm.

Elms are like ghosts to me.
Familiar,

but obscure. Absented from a modern
view of the world. Yet maintaining a thrall;
a haunting presence in my memory,
like something read about in a story.

A fungus called Dutch Elm Disease returned
in the sixties. Bark beetles imported
with a shipment of Canadian logs
carried the spores. In defence, our elms formed

tyloses which blocked their xylem. Stopping
water from reaching their leaves. Millions
died. Many were razed. Their tops lopped, or chopped
down from hedgerows to prevent transmission.

A visible cull. Giants embarrassed.
Reduced to mere shrubs.
The English Elm fared worst.
A genetically superior

super-elm. Imported by the Romans
and cloned. It had become
a monoculture. Sensitive to boom

and bust. And was massacred. Some species,

under ten metres, hidden on B-roads,
          were spared. Others were saved. Brighton Council
                instigated a superb survival
                      plan in the seventies and today boasts

          an elm filled town. Related to the nettle,
     elms are tenacious. They clone and sucker.
                Replicating from a root once the trunk
                      has been cut down. Creeping in to settle

docile woodland from the hedge. They will
     easily hybridise from their thick soup
                of genes. An evolutionary coup
                      that probably saved them before - in the

Neolithic when their population
          halved, but seemed to bounce back. Elms are brooding.
                Drawn to drowsiness or mortality.
                      Shedding rotten branches impatiently.

                Elm hateth man and waiteth, some would sing,

          back when we made coffins from their timber
     and pipes to drain mines or irrigate towns.

          I don't think it was that Saturday
          night, when I went night-swimming, that you died.

          It was probably Sunday night. When I
          did nothing memorable.

     You spoke to
your sister that Saturday night. Said you
          were proud of me graduating.

You died

in a crumpled heap at the bottom of
        the stairs. You were found on Monday morning
            by your kind neighbour. There was no warning.
                Just that stomach-ache and persistent cough.

    Rachael found out first. The police came round
to her flat. Sat her down. I'd turned my phone
    off. I honestly don't know why I did that.
        Usually I just turned down the sound.

But it was my friend Xim's drum performance
    and I didn't want my thigh vibrating.
            No-one important would ring. Later, rain
                teeming down pathetically, I switched

my phone back on and saw the words. *Ten missed
    calls*. I felt my stomach fall as I rang
        Rachael and we spoke.   Time frothed. Seemed to hang.
            Then drip off my coat. The rain beat and spat

on my shoulders. The force of   existence
    and not. I stood there. Hunched like a gargoyle
        in the building's long shadow. My joyful
            friend bounded towards me. *Pub?* he whispered.

    I nodded and followed. Still on the phone.
Muttering words. We thought you so stupid.

        Bloody minded. W*hy the hell did you do
            this?* Could you not tell us how you felt,

                                                loan

us some of your thoughts? We were glad of each
    other. Brother and sister. Knew we loved
        you and that the sadness would come. I cried

briefly outside the pub. Then went inside

to meet my friend's friend for the very first
time. It was better than being alone.
When I went home, Ben listened to the news.
Stunned. We needed to get out of the flat,

so, we walked up to Brent Lodge Park.
Found a bench in the dark.
Talked about old times.
And got drunk on cans.

We were saved from the rain by the bandstand.

3. A battered sycamore, Logan Rock

We approached the house. Your little Clio
on the gravel. You loved that stupid car,
     but still wished for a sleek, white Jaguar
and a home one could dance in with brio

     and voracity. We thought we'd break down,
when we got to the house. Our   childhood home.
     That your absence   would hit us.   Arouse
unstoppable emotions. That we'd drown

     in ruthless   tears. But it wasn't like that.
We went in and looked round. You weren't downstairs.
     Of course. But you could have been anywhere.
At work. Or out in the back garden. Sat

     on your bench, smoking a straight cigarette
and watching the ocean. On the kitchen
     table, someone had laid a card: *Darren
Saint, Funeral Director.* At least that's
     Sorted, I thought.

     In the small bedroom where you'd slept
     the sheets were crumpled.

     The light off.

     We stayed up until
two or three. Talking and listening to
     tunes. Remembering a time, only a
month before, when we last formed a triad.

     Deoxyribonucleic acid.

     A family.

Just you,   Rachael,   and me.
        We had driven out to see Logan Rock.
Parking near the pub where we used to go

        for Christmas Day drinks. The mossy green sign
said *Public Footpath*. But we knew the way.
        The route's been well worn since the eighty ton
balancing rock was tipped by two drunken

        sailors in eighteen-twenty-four. We walked
though ploughed fields, the path raised like a causeway.
        Helped you over stiles. Through clutching
                tendrils
        of bramble.
                Then past

        rogue pats of cow shit. Dropped like paint into
the loose brown soil. As we hoisted our legs
        over the ultimate granite lintel
we were surprised to see horses grazing

        on the cliffs. Equine necks bent to the task.
Their fat bellies silhouetted by a
        raw, meteoric sun hanging bulbous
in mid-arc, captivating the stunned blue

        sky, as the cliffs, cascading like rocky
waterfalls poured Cornwall into the sea.
        The wind played with the light. It was a day
to dry clothes outside.

                We were talking to

        stop the   ravenous march   of time.

        The next
morning we'd made an appointment at Treliske

hospital.

To   see   you.

                    We arrived early
and walked across the car park to Costa,

        buying tea we didn't want. Accosted
by thoughts, I spilt mine. Once I'd found tissues
        to clean up the mess, we were nearly late.
I couldn't remember when I'd said good-

        bye. Did you wave my train off from Penzance
as normal? The corridors slipped by as
        we followed the signs.   My thoughts were eclipsed.
It happened so quickly.   The nurse opened

        the door. You were there.   Your skin was waxy.
Bluish. Like glaucous leaves.   But not relaxed.
        Hard as bone.   Dead like bark. So it would crack
if you grew. But you can't.   Staged. A wooden

        actress playing the corpse of my mother.
A clearing.   Your scarred and bossed trunk lain stiff.
        Uprooted. Flat on your back wrapped in crisp
white sheets.   Felled.   An invasion begun long

        ago. The cancer, like   mycelium
strands, meandered   through your precious   heartwood,
        greenwood and bast.   Then grew, undiscovered,
in your pancreas epithelium.

        Eating you up.   Until all that   was left
was a shell.   And you fell.   Your blood glutted
        with sugar. Diabetic, like sap. Mud
            in your veins.

19

A turbulent knot of once peaceful grain.
The tears I was afraid would not come, came.

On those lonely cliffs near Logan
Rock, the horses are employed to grub out
        non-native sycamore which have settled
there, but are considered an invasion

from abroad. Horses eat the juvenile
green shoots to promote rare sea-lavender
        and vetch. Often confused with sycomore,
a fig species mentioned in the bible,

sycamore is a maple introduced
from Europe in the fifteenth century,
        that spectacularly naturalised.
This, the first tree I could identify,

is unpopular. They seed in gardens
where their roots upset houses and walls. Trains
        skid on their slippy mucilage - the wrong
sort of leaves. Their rampant growth is frowned on

by some conservationists. Despite claims
they boost worms and rare flowers. That flying
        insects love their nectar. Lichen their bark.
The West Cornwall peninsula would be

bereft without them. The only broadleaved
tree to survive the salt-laden gales that
        blow in off the rough seas. You loved the tracts
                of sycamores in Penwith and passed this

love on to me. I think that you admired
their outsider status. An immigrant
        with socialist tendencies. Mired in
idiosyncrasy and martyred by

adaptability. Resilient
in the face of a battering wind.
We dragged ourselves away from your bedside,
Went outside. Stood translucent in the sun

and watched the living bounce by. Back at yours,
I played my guitar to ease my troubles.
Rachael came in and sat down. She was still.
Just listening. Like you a month before.
Who wrote that? she asked, as the final chords
rang out.
I did, I said.
Oh, she said, w*ill*

you play it for us at the funeral?

4. A pulpit oak and an organ, Pendeen

That morning the sun rose. We dressed quickly,
    so that we could head up to Pendeen church
        for a soundcheck. Get back before
            the family arrived at the house.

The next Sunday was the harvest.
    The church windows were decorated with wheat
        and corn dollies. Aubergines and courgettes,
        reclined on the altar.

This bounty gave the building a pagan feel.
    It was perfect. So suggestive of you.
        Who never just embraced just one thing,
        but two.

    Grief soaked me. Struck me like a wave. Climate
        change. Tears came for a moment, then the tide,
        retreating,   rushed past my ankles,
      and away you went.

The Holme Seahenge was found when rotting
    tree stumps emerged from the sand.
        But, the seahenge is not a henge. It was used
        in the Bronze Age for excarnation.

Corpses lain on the inverted stump
    of a giant oak. Circled by spilt oakwood posts.
        Today, the venerable oak is vulnerable:
        to the changing tide of seasons and

temperature. To processionary

moths and caterpillars with toxic hair.
    To Acute Oak Decline and powdery mildew

which contribute stress to a dwindling
          population. If I am scared,

the oak is not. The King of the Woods dies
          standing up. Or lives on, stagheaded, crowned
                    with white boughs, supporting a carnival
                              of wildlife through lightning strikes. A symbol

          of survival. Of people. The English oak,
                    pedunculate; the Cornish dar, sessile.

The big black car skulked down the road.

Stopped dead by your house. My   body   froze
          for a   second. But I had to round up
          the relatives stood chattering in groups
                    in your living room. Not all in smart clothes.

You entered the church to loud opera:
          Mozart's Queen of the Night aria.
                    Your theme tune. Which we endured in the car
                              as children. Somersaulting sopranos

singing. The belly   of the nave was packed.
          We advanced past hunched   backs bent in silence
                    like greatcoated gravestones queuing for heaven,
                              bowed by your noise. Above us swelled the black

timber ribs supporting the white plaster
          roof, as if the building was holding its breath.
                    For a reclusive person you did well.
                              The community felt the disaster

of your passing and came. After the hymn,
          the prayers, a short sermon and eulogy -
                    which we carefully wrote and edited
over long emailed drafts - it was my turn.

I picked up my guitar. Loosened my tie.
    Played you *Sing me a Love Song* as I'd done
        in August. I am no singer.
            But that day in the church.

You lain beside me.
    The long box closed. All those quiet eyes
        upon us. The herring-bone parquet
        floor untrod.

The pulpit silent. The organ too.
    I found my voice.
        The melody ringing loud and true.
            That church, built for singing, both good news

and the blues, resonated like timber.
    The lyrics sung. Not for them. But for you.
        Then the last sound faded. The spruce soundboard
        of my Martin guitar, damped by the stern

hand of a trillion airborne particles,
    was still. I sat for a moment, breathing.
        Staring out at the room.

I saw lignin.

Dead wood.

A world made of trees. Paper and hymn books.
    Your conifer coffin. The gentle pine pews.
        But oak dominated.
            Black timbers on the walls.

Cut blocks on the floor.
    Turned scrolls on the pulpit.
        The organ flaunting golden trunks.

The oak's robust wood has built this island.

Supported the institutions of government
and debate. The roughhewn pillars
inside a Neolithic longhouse.
The hammerbeam roof of Westminster Hall.

Oak too, bore sailors through turbulent seas.
The Brigg Logboat hacked out of a single
fifty-foot trunk in one-thousand BC.
Drake's flagship the Golden Hind. Cut from oak

and caulked in tar. Sailed from Plymouth sound
to Palau. Via California.
With piracy, slavery and colonialism,
those less admirable island traditions,

packed in the hold with the guns and the crew.
I once saw Henry's gaudy warship,
the Mary Rose, lying in state in her
brand new glass case at Portsmouth docks. We
mark

time in great ages of stone, bronze and iron.
In steel, then plastic. But those arthritic
spars. The curling tusks of near crumbled oak
raised from the depths of the ocean, revealed

something else to me. That wood parallels
all human history. And just like us
will disappear. But for exceptional
cases. Into the dusty past.

Four boys carried you.

The coffin on our shoulders. We walked down
the aisle to Radiohead's Creep. Your

25

favourite song. When   Johnny
Greenwood's angry guitar   stabs ripped sonic

holes in Thom   Yorke's beatific C minor
      chord my free hand clenched   as if you had kicked
         the coffin wall   and I felt that   if you
were asleep, you weren't any more.

The professionals took over when we
      reached the door. So that Rachael and I could
         both follow you. One last time. From the church
to dad's grave. A journey as familiar as

our own garden path. All those Sundays
      and Christmases we'd walked it with you.
         We arrived at dad's wounded plot. All opened up.
The five feet of loam that maintained a distance

between you. Removed. Thick, twisted ropes slid
      through the undertaker's grip. Lowered
         your body into the ground. There, it joined
your heart which had been interred beside him

      since nineteen-eighty-nine. Perhaps apart
from the battered remnant, ventricle, or
      atrium, which you kept alive just for
Rachael and I.
         We were loved from the start,

until that grave day when you breathed your last.

5. A sprig of holly, Bristol

Christmas felt different. Rachael invited
me to Bristol. That much was tradition.
As we always did it. But little else.

     I stayed in a hotel by the Bear Pit

and woke alone. The cheap sheets rough on my
cheek. I showered. Packed up my things. Walked down
for breakfast. Down flat, empty corridors.
A hollow stairwell. Twelve echoing stairs.

By the reception desk, a library
of leaflets. Hoar white walls.
She might have smiled.

     The receptionist might have smiled.

The dining room. A bain-marie buffet.
The smell of warmed food. Three televisions
flicked through random pictures like silent card
dealers shuffling cards. A blue-eyed news

reader mouthed words. A rectilinear
cavern. An alien outpost, bipeds
bent over plates. A sprig of holly stuck
to the corner of a watercolour

print of the sea. I wasn't even sure
it was real. I once tried to find some wild
holly in the woods. I went to Windsor
like a poacher. To scavenge and search.

     To find it uncultivated. To bring

it home. A fresh green branch with red berries.
The female bears berries. I found holly
in the underwood. Tree after tree. None

wore jewellery. Where had that berried sprig
come from? From what planet did the hotel
buy its holly? I served myself breakfast.
Dolloped beans on my plate. Laid down slices

of bacon like patches of rubbery
skin. The tray clacked against the hard plastic
table. No one looked up. Feeders: coupled
or alone. That morning I saw Christmas

unclothed. A white, empty, calendar square.
One stroke of a knife-scored tally scarring
the soft verglas of a prison cell wall.

            Where was the mistle thrush?

The mistle thrush guards the red crop
proprietorially, like a proud farmer.
Guards the red berries. The green leather leaves.
I wanted to see fox and deer stroll through the room.

Browse the remnants of breakfast dumped
like faeces on the evacuated
tables. Holly protects itself with spiked
leaves.

            Collecting Holly hurts. There is blood.

Crimson drops of blood welling up on whorled
fingertips. But, high up, above the lippy
reach of grazing deer, or snatching human
paws, the leaves are smooth. Spikes are expensive

and holly is an accountant. The Scrooge
of Christmas. An evolutionary
cost-benefit analyst. Slike holly
has spineless leaves. No good for Christmas then.

We want berries and spikes. Things have to be
right. But then, sometimes, even that is not
enough. It seemed that everything had been
lost with you gone. Like a tree cut down. Nests

and leaves, sinking into the loam.

Why can't we talk about trees?
I want to talk
about trees.

We used to meet in Bristol at Christmas.
Rent an apartment. Have drunken lunches
and shop in charity shops. My leather
jacket lay beside me on the plastic

chair. I'd bought it the last time I was there
with you. My mobile buzzed.

Skated sideways

on the rime of the table. The lit screen
shimmered. *Merry Christmas gorgeous.*

Sunrise warmed the icy glacier.

If I had not met Caroline at that Halloween
party I don't know what I would have done.

It was too late for you. Halloween. You
won't meet her now. I remember seeing
you in Clifton in the black and white cold.

Bare branches. Frosty grass. The bridge where we

saw the cave. High on the cliff face. The maw
of the gorge. The long drop to the icy
water below. You would have liked to live
in Clifton. You could have sold the house, bought

a flat. But you wouldn't move away from
Cornwall. Away from that semi-detached
house with the view of the sea where dad died.

   We argued. So, I stopped talking to you

about it.

   I was there. At yours. I was so angry. I had to smash a picture
   (not one of dad's) into the wall so that the frame splintered
   and black nails rained over the cream carpet like seeds.

I walked up to Rachael's.

Up the deserted Gloucester Road. Skull and
crossbones and a topsy-turvy Jesus
for company. Graffiti adorned walls.
The hollow eyes of derelict buildings.
Neon posters pasted onto the cracked

glass of old phone boxes advertised gigs.
I carried a big bag of wrapped presents.
A beaming, red-cheeked Santa swinging
by my calf muscles.

I looked for holly. Holly takes root
anywhere. In the crucks of an oak.
A dirty pyramid in the corner
of a wrecked booth. In the shade.
         Underwood.

Holly. Ilex. Holly. Ilex. Holly.

I once thought it a bush. That signpost tree.
That boundary tree. Perpendicular
branches pointing. Marker of the secret
subterranean tin lodes. A single

trunk. The whitest wood. In her flat Rachael
had put up real holly and mistletoe.
Brought in the outside. A bauble-laden
tree. Titus was swimming in a sea of

ripped wrapping paper. Hugs. Tall, cava-filled
glasses. I felt like an invader. Like
holly in the home. Spiked. Temporary.

Uncomfortably wedged between cushions

of leather furniture. Despite the food
I felt empty. Another glass. The day
felt empty. *Cheers*. A gesture. Like an old
village church. Holly hung for the solstice.

The original Cornish Christmas tree.
I could hear your voice singing. *The holly
and the ivy, when they are both full grown.*
For fertility. Continuity

of life. From before written time. Before
Christianity. Our only native
evergreen. Eight-thousand BC. I could
hear you singing. *In the bleak midwinter.*

Easily adopted into the new
religion. A gateway tree. From the branch
to the cross. The oak to holly. *The blood*

of Christ keep us in eternal life. Red

drops. The berries dripping from that spiny
crown of emerald thorns. I made a sort
of shrine in my bedroom back in London.
I don't normally hang photographs.

I live in my head. But I dug out some
frames. It was Rachael's idea. Every
time I came home. Or when I awoke. Your

    presence shocked me. A jolt. Reminded

    me that I would never see you again.

It was like in Cornwall. Going to yours.
People had sent cards. I was not prepared
for that. Those envelopes arriving to
an empty house. Piling on the doormat.

We lined the cards up on the long kitchen
windowsill amongst your fossils. Your pens.
Your classical plaster busts. And the gold
teeth you'd didn't seem to want to part with.

It was where we would put birthday cards. They
looked like birthday cards. If you didn't
read the words. *Apology. Loss. Sorry.*
Condolence.

    Apology. Loss. Sorry.

        Condolence.

  Sympathy.
      Thinking

of you.

        Heartfelt.

   Deepest

          Sympathy.

We could have hung up some holly instead.

To guard us from evil. From spirits. From
death. Place holly in the house. Holly
in the byre. Holly along the hedges
to prevent a witch from passing. We could

have knocked on wood. Take a bough but never
the entire tree. It brings bad luck to fell
a holly tree. After Christmas we tried
to dismantle your house. Our childhood home.

We didn't know where we should start. Each lamp
a symbol. Each chair a sigil. Your books
held a narrative. Spoke of you. It was
impossible to move. Impossible

      to touch. As if touching one thing would,
like a card pulled from the base,
            collapse the whole
    house,
       so that everything in it,
the dust packed in the nooks,
      stuck in the crannies, would blow
                away.

And when the wind dropped, you'd be gone.

6. A willow on the bank, Brentford

January must have happened because

February came - when the Celts remove
holly from their homes. Turn their eyes to spring.
I had to leave my freezing flat. Get out.
London was grey. Even the sky. Even

the towpath. I walked along the canal.
The confluence of the Grand Union
with the Brent river. The final tidal
rush to the Thames. Three quick miles. Fast after

the stagnant snake, horse pace from Birmingham
On the banks. A gallery of: crack,
sallies, withy, weeping, saugh, sauchen, white,
osier, goat, pussy, sallow, cricket

bat willow. The water was mottled: green,
black, silver, brown. Deep and dank. A sheet pulled
over the beds of the locks. Hanwell's flight
of locks. The giant beams of the gate arms

protruded acutely, oars from the hull
of the canal - each clanking as if slung
on metal outriggers. Sunblacked shadows
of leafless branches. The path footbruised, tyre-

scarred, muddy. I walked alone. A slender
heron perched on a chipped timber tooth flew
off with lazy wafts of its pewter wings.
And just then I thought
I am a trunk
struck by axe blows
of sorrow.

The steep, humpbacked spine
of the bridge lay like a bell curve across
the canal. I walked alone. I'd pushed them
away. People: Rachael, Caroline, Ben.

People. All getting in my way. Talking.
Wanting to talk. Or offering to talk.
Checking in. Death is silent. Did they not
know? A liberty of silence. Freedom.

Crack willow cracks. CRACK.
The branch, twig, bough, wing, wood, sprig, prong, splits.
Floats
down the river. Roots. Sprouts. Shoots. Clones itself.
Propagates. Replicates in another

location. I was walking fast. With quick
feet and long London strides. Brushing brambles
aside. Warm. Energised. Impatiently
waiting for a large family of cyclists

to pass. At once peaceful and occupied.
Noisy and silent. The Brent is semi -
tidal. Canalised. Made navigable
for: narrowboats, punts, barges, scows, flatboats,

low draft freight ships. Trains took the business
away. Left the waterways to: idlers,
gazers,   fisherfolk, walkers, gongoozlers
like me. And just then I thought
Getaway from me
go I am ugly
the red pain will stain.

Elixirs
of willow bark: hot, bitter infusions,

teas, potions, brews, libations. Drunk to ease:
fever, deliriums, temperatures,

tremors, chills, ague. Chewed to calm: toothache, holes,
throbbings, twinges, cavities, headaches, deep
migraines. Salicylic acid. Bayer
synthesised Aspirin. I walked on through

the apocalyptic landscape of mud
shadows and abandoned water-logged tents
underneath the M4 motor way.
I was somehow glad you

were not there. In my head. On my shoulders.
The pressures of: support, love's judgement,

to talk to you. Gone. A Piccadilly
line train screamed over the red-tinged metal

bridge, fraught, as if some terrible missile.
Osterley lock. Clitheroe lock.
Brentford Gauging Locks. By the time I reached
the Double Thames Lock, number one hundred

and one, I was exhausted.
The light patchy, part of it missing.
The air grainy, the bank pixillated,
paddling ducks animated.

I wanted to believe in the
religious fantasy of creation,
where things emerge easily. Ideas
manifest, each perfectly formed. In stark

contrast to our reality which takes
a near impossible effort to build.
Osier poles, wands, withy, wicker, pleached,

woven and plashed, warp over weft,

under-wreathed, meshed. To make baskets, cradles,
bassinets, swills, panniers, and creels; sound
screens for motorways, reinforced river
banks, gargantuan puppets at Lafrowda
Day, St Just.

I could not go back home.
Far too cold in the flat. I remembered
I'd once seen my friend,
play in a pub somewhere

near Brentford. I found It on Google Maps.
The Brewery Tap. I wondered if there
was any live music happening that
night. It was Friday in London. The pub

was quiet. But a man in a Stetson
was setting up a mic stand. A guitar
leant in the corner like a dunce. I asked,
is there music? He said,

why, do you play?
I said *sometimes*. He said,
what, like tonight?
It's an open mic.

I said, *cool. OK.*

I didn't even have my guitar.

He scrawled my name on a scrap of paper
and smiled. *Good to have you along.* And just
then I thought
I bark I froth I
spitandclaw don't dare

talk to me

SNAP
canine
        teeth closeonyourarm.

        I nursed a pint for two hours
    so as not to get drunk. I watched Scotland
play France in the Six Nations on my phone.
Anything not to get drunk.

    The Guinness Clock

ticked. He tuned his guitar. Then placed it back
        in the corner. France tried, Scotland won. My
                pint glass was half full. And then half empty.
    I went to the toilet. When I came back

        I was greeted by amplified guitar
    and banter. Thank God. He played some: Dylan
            Cash, Cline, Baez, Peter Green. The pub filled
                up. Guitars lay prone on pew-like benches.

        A man with a blue cap and white bushy
    beard plucked the strings of a mandolin. Two
            Staffies sniffed round my feet for food. Players
waved at their friends and I moved my coat

    so a couple with a taut tambourine
and loose maracas could sit. He played some
        Elvis. Something else. I was too nervous.
            It was getting obvious that I would

    have to play. *This was a mistake. I should
probably go home.* The sound of leather
            on willow. The sight of Arthur Rackham's
                drawings for Wind in the Willows, grey buds

38

furred, cats' paws, goslings. He whispered, *you're next.*
After these two do their turn. A couple
of songs. That OK? I nodded mutely.
Insides churning. I closed my eyes. I drilled

myself. I had practised. I loved this. *Take*
this opportunity. My heart clattered
on my ribs like a gurney on cobbles.
I wiped my clammy hands on my blue jeans,

faded, muddy. My hair was so greasy.
I'd not showered for days.
Welcome. Lawrence,
he said. And I could hear my voice coming

through the PA.
And I could not believe
it was my voice. I kept thinking of you
as I sung. Of course. I played *Rapeseed, Ogres*

and *Long Lost Rover.* They all clapped. Not
politely. A lot. Shook my hand. This had
not ever happened before. Before, when
I played, people drank and talked. What had changed?

I staggered back to my seat. I got asked
to play again. So I played *Sing me a Love*
Song. And the pub, like the church, was silent.
I got drunk. I walked off to the bus stop

and ignored all the texts and missed calls on
my phone. Why would they not listen? The black
river of tarmac was warmed by the glow
of amber streetlights. Time to go home.

And just then I thought: I miss you.

Over the tundra,
valleys, moorland, steppe, plateaus, heath, tracts, shires,
of England came the arctic trees: sallow,
willow, aspen. birch. Pioneer species.

Fast growing. Short-lived. The birth of wildwood.
Eleven thousand years before Jesus.
The willow's crown is patchy. Full of: holes,
gaps, vents, chinks, tunnels, runnels, light. It too

is colonised. Nurtures a small woodlet
of: ash, holly, gooseberry, elder, fern,
honeysuckle and bramble.
The red bus stopped

by the shelter. I climbed aboard, tapped my
card on the reader, found a seat.
I thought
I was happy in the pub. But I had just
forgotten.
The bus
jerked forwards.
The head of a boy, asleep in a hoodie,
flopped onto his chest, broken necked.

I had never felt more alone.

7. An amputated London plane, West Ealing

The next day,
            after trying to teach maths, I walked home
        from the Tube. From Boston Manor up to
            Hanwell.
Pulled out my phone. This would be
                    a good time.   We could talk. As I

    Then I remembered. There was no one there. At first your
        voicemail only said your name.

                Judith

        Then that too was
                    deleted. Your number disconnected.

        The beeps of the dead.

At military intervals I passed a London Plane tree
guarding the streets. They are autotrophs, self-feeders.
Hard workers. Contributing. Cleaning the air.

Providing shade. Reducing the urban heat island effect.
They are indifferent to pruning. Exfoliate. Shed bark. Grime
washes off their leathery leaves. Their two-tone trunk,

is grey and green. Camouflage. Vitiligo. They are
uncomplaining. Cages around their roots.

                You worked. You had to.
She had you unloading
            the boot of her car

    on that last day. Lugging

and dragging. Just a month before.
        Big cases onto the gravel.
                You, who was carrying so much shit already.
            Just a month before you died.

Some lads were staring.
        I think they were laughing at me.
                Sat at my computer.
                        In my
            work shirt and smart trousers. They didn't know

        I was writing.   They thought I
was an accountant. Like I would have been
        had I not quit university. The
            first time. I am sorry. I am
            not sorry.

I was in the pub. I hadn't gone home.
        The football was on. I had got drunk. I was
typing up some poetry. To excuse my
        drinking. My phone was buzzing and buzzing.

Caroline. Trying to get hold of me.
        Find out if I was OK. The black phone
        radiating light across the dark wood
of the table. She was trying to reach

me through the darkness. A deep sea
        angler fish.
            The lantern is a lure.

                Fuck off.

        I put the phone into my pocket. The missed

The messages. I hoped it wouldn't bite
my leg off. I ignored it. I hated
it. It loved me and needed me so I

hated it even more. Fuck off.
Where did the anger come
from? There was a forest of it inside me.
But I

didn't switch my phone off. Not after last time.

Someone important
might have called.

But you didn't call.

I phoned Rachael a lot around that time,
Late nights stood under a canopy of
five trees. On the herringbones. Alone. Just
outside the yellow-red flare of the Shell

garage. Where the brokenstreet light sucked dark
like a missing tooth. Drinking cans of beer.
Smoking. One hour. Two. We talked
to pretend we understood.
Discussing ways of getting on.

Applying science.

This is no time to be emotional.

We must pollard and coppice.
Sometimes we must cage the roots.
Girdle the trees. To stay
in control. We must stay in control of
nature. Nature is chaos. Dark matter.

                                    Empty
spaces.

Not knowing.
            Random bifurcation.
                    We know for sure a leaf will fall
                            but we don't know which one.

        How could I miss
you when you lived somewhere else?
                            Nothing there had changed. You were not

    But you never were.
                    I wanted to disappear.
                            I wanted to drink. To drown.

    I had an
            urge in me to. To
                    disappear. I ordered another pint.
    Then went   outside.

    I have disappeared into the night.
            This is a different world now.

                    The city is
                        shapes. Not substance.

                            I have been hanging out with the laughing
        lads. Drinking and drinking. Shadows

    and voids. We're on the canal.
                    The geometric river.
                            The arc
                    of the tunnel. A negative

quadratic.

Mathematics is so peaceful. So unworldly. Problems can
                    be solved. A language of peace. I can solve
            the problems.

                    Teachers have failed at something.

    I can't get it out of my head.

                    The silvered water is sliced acutely
                by
            the tunnel's
        shadow like a   guillotine
blade. Recessed
                into naked darkness.

    Three of us looking for drugs.

                        Negative

                                            spaces.

                        The far bank
                        is vertical.
                        A thick
                        black cliff.

                Yellowed lamplight bites a scalene
            triangle out of the dark tow path. Four
                        shadows.
            By the low wall.

    We wait. A new man comes. We wait. The new
                    man is twice my size. His coat is puffed-puffed. His

bones are wide-wide.
His face is swollen. He is twice my

We smoke a cigarette to pass the time.
The night is planes
and lines.

Mathematics.
If you see it. London plane
trees and train lines. If you want to see
it that way.

Plane trees are monoecious,
hermaphrodite, but are selected to be more male.

More male branches. Less pollen.
Less seed. Less seedpods. Less of the mess
of creation. Less menstruation. To be easier

to maintain. But the pollen is an allergen. Hay
fever. Rashes. The short, stiff hairs. Trichomes
shed by young leaves get up the nose.
There's sneezing.
Things to put up your nose.

There is a short
path off the canal. The path slopes

upwards.
Between two
monochrome walls. Red
in the day. The night is

winter. The colour absconded. Only
shapes remain. Square latticed bricks. Sparse rectangles.
Stretcher-brick-bond. A shadow comes. We palm

the bag. We're gone. You know all about my life.

Well nearly all.

More than I knew about yours.

We are locked in a box. In a bedroom.
The three of us. Me, him
and the other.

A bed and a stereo. Posters on the

Lines. White powder
up my nose. I am

dancing like I am boxing.
Fists up

by my face.

The music is low.

We can barely
hear it. He is lying on the bed. *Be quiet,*

he says. *Shh.*

It's his house. It's his

dad's house. A man moves
in the corridor.

Shut the fuck up, he

Laughing.   Lines.   Drum

and bass.

The music is quiet
but we can hear it. Voices talk behind
the closed door.

The closed door.

In the closed corridor.
                    In the kitchen.
                    Steps and voices.   A girl's.   A

In our box
            we dance. Swaying. Hands
clenched
                    up by my face. I am
            a London Plane. Pollarded. Clubbed
                    hands. *Psycho Fighter.* Stumps as if boxing
                            gloved. Or amputated. I am
            shaking
my fists at the sky. An amber ceiling
            of light.
                                        So

            high.
I am outside myself looking down.

            The London Plane regains its crown
            if its head gets chopped off. The final
            wish of Anne Boleyn. Achieved by a tree.

            Many of our trees will regrow when their
            extremities are lopped. No one knows why.
            Or how. Green shoots shooting up from raw stumps.

            Trees massing,   spreading wide,   multi-trunked,
            ancient dodderels,   coppiced and   pollarded, lengthening
            their life span to thousands of

            A brutal cut. The branches. Some trunk,
            some heartwood. A maiden is one uncut.
            In a world named by men.

            The roots are the tree. Not what

we see above. There is evidence for the art of coppicing going back
six thousand years.

                                        The other sits at
                    a desk.
            Playing with a bank card.

Cutting
            up
                        lines. On the otherside of the room

we talk about our
                        mums. He and I. About
                                    those who have died.
                You came here to talk, he says.
            We shake hands. Sweaty hands. The other
                        passes the mirror. Last lines. The

            is gone.
Hours have passed in a moment.
                                    He has to work tomorrow. He is a
                    gardener.
                                    We say,
    plant us some flowers. Plant us a tree.
                                    Fuck off now, he says.
                                    The two of us walk downwind

to a twenty-four hour

There is an inflorescence of boys
stood by the hairdressers. Closed. Shutters up.
                Hoods up. We are high. We are all out in

        the middle of the night. Conversation
comes easily. In ten minutes
                    we have bought some weed.

He wants to talk.
One of the boys with a kind face.
                    Smiling. *Somali*, he says,

                                        you? He wants to talk to us white
                    boys.
He sees

    an opportunity
                    for something. We want to talk
    to him. He says,
                    I know where you can smoke.
                                        Not here. Too many
police.

                                        We are on the main road.
                                        We follow
                                        him.

Platanus crossed Hispanica. The London Plane is a
hybrid. Offspring of the oriental and western
planes. Two trees that would never have met in the wild.

                                        The boy
                                        leads us down a side street.

The London Plane was brought from Spain.

                                        He stands
                                        under the looming wall
                                        of a closed Sainsbury's super
                    market.

The London Plane was first cultivated in Clapham
by John Tradescant the Younger.

And presses a dimly lit button
on the sheer cliff of brick.

The London Plane was originally crossed in the botanic
garden of Oxford University in the seventeenth century.

Nooneknows.

The lift comes. *They
don't switch it off,* he says.
So this is where we go when it rains. The lift

goes up.

We

step out

onto the deserted grey

plateau of the car free car park. Then we go

and sit in the stairwell.
Cocooned.
As if inside the trunk
of a tree. We roll
joints.
He doesn't smoke.
We're talking like a gale. Words flying,
spiralling
like leaves.
Multiplying like cultivars of the
London Plane: Augustine Henry Bloodgood, Metroshade *Life is fucking
amazing sometimes,* Columbia, *That we can be here, Like this,* Liverty,
Pyrimidalis, *We could solve the world's problems right here,* Metzam, *If we just sat
down together,* Mirkovec, *We are doing this now, This is equality,* Yarwood, *Things
that look very different but are actually the same, This is mathematics,*

We
are
here.

I slowly opened my eyes. It was light
outside, the curtains glowing red. By my
          head the angle-poise lamp. Its hundred watt
bulb pointed at my face. Humming.

A second sun.

When gaslights first arrived on
the streets of England, unburnt ethylene,
          a hormone, caused the street trees to lose their
leaves. Now, streetlights prompt trees to keep their

          leaves for longer on the side nearest the
lamp. Every tree is adapted to
          the idea that long days are warm and short
days are cold. Everything, all they do -

          germination, abscission, dormancy,
the production of flowers and cones - is
          based upon this assumption. Perhaps soon
this evolved assumption will no longer

          be valid. What then? The confusion of
city trees under lights is a warning.
          My phone started to ring. *Hi, Caroline.
Yeah, I'm OK.*
          But that wasn't true.
                                   At all.
          I started to cry. *I'm sorry.*
The pillow
          was wet.
                    I'm sorry.

Go, she said, *you need to go.*

To Cornwall she meant.   To be near you.

And I knew she was right.

8. Rowan pollen, Chysauster

later... sitting on a train

winging above a steel arc
across blue-skied Wiltshire to Cornwall

pressing my forehead
to the vibrating glass

the rushing track
a mutable slate river

shimmying hypnotically below
the gravel scree

blurring
pulsing beneath me

at dizzying speeds
looking up

seeing dismembered JCBs
bereft of shovels

resting their club wrists
on the ground of a lithic breakers yard

like marooned broken birds
trampolines and moth-eaten

mattresses lurking in
back gardens like burglars

earlier... hanging up the phone

rising slowly from my bed

opening the curtains
and knowing that I needed to see you

the day streaming in like
a crowd down a platform

particles of sunlight
your face not among them

standing in my hallway
five exits:

kitchen living-room bathroom bedroom
the darkness rising from down the stairs

        a waterfall
        four mossy rocks

        a rowan tree guarding the threshold
        between this world and the next

how many doorways
gateways and exits

standing between Hanwell and Pendeen
between my flat and your grave

        said to be the tree upon which
        the Devil hanged their mother

quickly booking a train on my phone
it only cost

money

sending short emails saying

I wouldn't be in for teaching
for the foreseeable

future
thinking unforeseeable future

        rowan from rountree from Old
        Norse reynir for red

packing a bag
stuffing a bag

with clothes for that week
heading down

the water-dark stairs
closing the door to my flat

        the wayfarer's tree
        preventing those on a journey from getting lost

standing in the dark corridor
between my flat

and London
an indeterminate space

of unvacuumed carpet
and piles of post

addressed to people
who didn't live there anymore

        old English cwic-beam

became quickbeam

became cwic, wick and from
that wicken the witch tree

dialectical variants
folk etymology

locking the external door
with the great Yale key

treading the conveyor belt pavement
to the station

through the tile-arched tunnel
under the tracks

if a bird drops a sticky rowan seed
into a fork of an oak or a maple it may grow

as an epiphyte on the larger tree
a flying rowan

remembering your rituals
tying a wreath

onto the headstone for dad at Christmas
with white string

a flying rowan
a witch

realising this is how it's done
feeling a need to leave

something on your grave
to give me a reason to go

to say to myself that I am here with you
never understanding

this need before
understanding it now

        there is a pentagram mark on their berries
        on the opposite side to the stalk

the barriers at Paddington
easing open

like nut shells in autumn
the heavy door of Costa resisting

my urge
me leaning on it more than opening it

so that it held me up
in weightless equilibrium

        apotropaic magic
        gargoyles on churches

        figureheads on ship
        deflecting evil

        get thee behind me, Satan
        get death out of my house

the doors hissing in between the carriages
sighing like the attempt to exhale

heartache
trying to find an unreserved seat

on an empty train
leaving the station

> rowan chosen for the mantel
> rowan carved for the chimney breast

remembering you waving me off from
Penzance when I first came to London

just a slim pencil of clothing and
paper skin scorched by the sun

what did you do once I had gone
when you were alone again

> rowan twigs above doorways
> tied around the necks of cows

every time I leave
a room or a train station

you seem to die
every time I remember you

you die again
remorseless this

> rowan cut for pocket charms against
> rheumatism

crossing the M25
a grey belt holding in the sweating

obesity of London
protecting the city from the countryside

        we pretend we are safe
        that we are in control

        that we will not die
        the rowan is susceptible to fireblight

remembering the Iron Age
settlement at Carn Euny

going down into the fogou
with you

a souterrain
buried like a secret

or treasure or happiness
in the aftermath of sadness

going down the cobbled slope
running

into that cold chamber buried
for storage or habitation or ritual

        we do not know
        will never know

you somewhere behind
huddling chthonic

our family of three in the cold underground
no devils here

just absence
and questions

just history
you loved Carn Euny

        rowan pollen was found
        buried at Chysauster

        the other settlement
        ten miles away

you never liked
Chysauster

as much
it did not have a fogue

and had a proper car park
so was much more popular

        before sixteen hundred
        trees were not really planted

        the landscape was defined
        by the trees found there

        stone circles built near
        the rowan trees

        not the other way around
        the world not defined afterwards

        by planting
        by men

the train passing over the Tamar bridge hanging
between the valley sides

an empty cage waiting for a train
it will never catch

        rowan is now a street tree
        planted indiscriminately without meaning

        this does not mean there are more
        gateways

        all it means is that people
        are disconnected from landscape

        and rowan has spread like a weed
        through the edgeland

St Austell
Par Truro

Camborne Redruth
sprouting up everywhere

        like the ghost of you roaming those places
        searching for an exit

locking myself in the toilet to stop time passing
bouncing along in a private box

staring at yellowing plastic walls
changing only imperceptibly

        fid na ndruad wizard's tree

mountain ash kerdhynen

the many named rowan
is not an ash despite

the similarity between
their pinnate leaves

arriving at yours and finding
a locked door

I had not thought about
the locked door

we never used to lock up
even when you weren't in

finding a key in the garage
and sighing with relief

the rowan is a *Sorbus* like whitebeam
and the wild service tree

is easily confused with
the true service tree

or the other way
round

letting myself in
to the empty house

removing the condolence cards
from the windowsill

they did not remind me

of you

they only reminded me of the funeral when
you were someone else

the next day, when I had my courage up
winding my way to the graveyard

to say goodbye